RHYME'S REASON

JOHN HOLLANDER

Rhyme's Reason

A Guide to English Verse

NEW HAVEN AND LONDON
YALE UNIVERSITY PRESS

Designed by Nancy Ovedovitz and set in VIP Palatino type.
Printed in the United States of America by The Alpine Press, Stoughton,
Mass.

Library of Congress Cataloging in Publication Data
Hollander, John.
  Rhyme's reason.

  Bibliography: p.
  1. English language—Versification. I. Title.
PE1505.H6   821'.009   81-51342
ISBN 0-300-02735-4   AACR2
ISBN 0-300-02740-0 (pbk.)

10 9 8 7 6 5 4 3 2 1

Portions of this book were published earlier, as pages 575–96 in *Literature as Experience*, by Irving Howe, John Hollander, and David Bromwich, copyright © 1979 by Harcourt Brace Jovanovich, Inc., and are reprinted with permission.

For Lizzy and Martha

Chosen illustrations of form get dafter
As they shy from *Familiar Quotations*;
Most examples follow too slowly after
        Their explanations,

Though even if I could improve the timing
There's no one I could trust to do the graphics
And so, even as now I do in rhyming
        Horace's sapphics,

Scorning such an account of rhyme as uses
Assembly-line quotations, then, I fill a
Book with verses handmade, the sterner Muses'
        Laughing ancilla.

CONTENTS

his is a guide to verse, to the formal structures which are a necessary condition of poetry, but not a sufficient one. The building blocks of poetry itself are elements of fiction—fable, "image," metaphor—all the material of the nonliteral. The components of verse are like parts of plans by which the materials are built into a structure. The study of rhetoric distinguishes between tropes, or figures of meaning such as metaphor and metonymy, and schemes, or surface patterns of words. Poetry is a matter of trope; and verse, of scheme or design. But the blueprints of verse can be used to build things made of literal, or nonpoetic material—a shopping list or roadside sign can be rhymed—which is why most verse is not poetry.

It is nonetheless common and convenient for most people who don't read carefully to use "poetry" to mean "writing in some kind of verse," and to regard thereby the design without considering the materials. The most popular verse form in America today—the ubiquitous jingle readers identify with "poetry" even as, fifty or sixty years ago, they did anything that rhymed—is

a kind of free verse
without any special
constraints on it except
those imposed by
the notion—also
generally accepted—that
the strip the lines
make as they run
down the page (the
familiar strip with the
jagged
right-hand edge) not
be too wide

1

This is as automatic and unpoetic in its arbitrary formality as jingling rhymes on "June" and "moon" ever were; schemes and structures of free verse are as conventional and, for most writers, as "academic" as certain other "official" forms have been in other eras. Major poetry has been built in this form, even as Tennyson could employ the same rhyming schemes as writers of occasional verses for family parties.

Both verse and prose, then, are schematic domains. Literacy used to entail some ability to write in both modes, without any presumption of poetry in the execution of skill in the former. But today sportswriters on the few newspapers we have left know no Latin nor can write good witty verses. We no longer memorize poems at school. Young persons are protected from the prose cadences—so influential on writing in both modes—of the King James Bible by aggressive separatism and the churches themselves; all of us are shielded from Shakespearean rhythm by the ways in which both prose and verse are publicly intoned in America. The territory covered in this guide—this road map through the region of poetry in English—has itself tended to run back into second-growth timber, if not into wilderness.

Some day we will all be reading Blue Guides and Baedekers to what once were our own, familiar public places. In former times, the region of verse was like an inviting, safe municipal park, in which one could play and wander at will. Today, only a narrow border of that park is frequently used (and vandalized), out of fear that there is safety only in that crowded strip—

even as the users' grandparents would cling to walks that went by statues—and out of ignorance of landscape. The beauties of the rest of that park are there, unexplored save by some scholars and often abandoned even by them.

I am old enough to have grown up in the park, and to map a region one loves is a way of caressing it. (Goethe wrote of counting out hexameters on his Roman lady's back as she lay in his arms: he was mapping her body's curve even as he felt for the ancient rhythm.) I too set out now as a loving rather than merely dutiful tour guide. Even today, when touch seems casual and only discourse intimate, one can't presume on Whitmanic relations with readers. I shall content myself (Inquiry's too severe in prose; / Verse puts its questions in repose) with tapping out my self-explaining diagrams and illustrations of the walks and alleys and bosks and ponds and parterres and follies and hahas and so forth that comprise my territory, as it were, on the reader's hand. After all, this *is* a manual.

The schemes and designs to be explored here include: the structures of lines of verse; patterns of rhyme, alliteration, and assonance; schemes of syntax and word order; groups of lines called strophes or stanzas; overall patterns of repetition and variation (refrains, etc.); and larger arrangements of these. Over the centuries, these forms have come at various times to be associated with one or another kind of poetic use—or with what some critics would call a "theme," a "subject" or an occasion. Sonnets, for example, start out by being about a particular philosophic conception of love, and end up in the twentieth century as descriptions of pictures, explanations of myths, or analytic meditations. And yet the later poems in the history of the form's life—when written by the finest poets—are always in some way aware of, and always engage, that history and the burden it puts on originality.

This little book contains examples of formal schemes of various sorts, and at various levels of organization. Since we are concerned only with verse in English, no historical sketch or comparative analysis of metrics and forms is given, save for a glance at what the meters of classical poetry have entailed for English. But it should be remembered that all poetry was originally oral. It was sung or chanted; poetic scheme and musical pattern coincided, or were sometimes identical. Poetic form as we know it is an abstraction from, or residue of, musical form, from which it came to be divorced when writing replaced memory as a way of preserving poetic utterance in narrative, prayer, spell, and the like. The ghost of oral poetry never vanishes, even though the conventions and patterns of writing reach out across time and silence all actual voices. This is why, to go back to the earlier analogy of architecture, a poet is always like both the builder of houses, with plans "at hand," and the designer or executor of a complicated edifice, drawing and working from complex blueprints.

Verse can be organized according to very many metrical *systems*, depending upon the structure of the language in which the verse is written. The systems relevant to verse in English are:

1. *Pure accentual*—the meter of the earliest Germanic poetry; it is preserved in nursery rhymes and in much lyric verse.

2. *Accentual-syllabic*—the verse system which involves such patterns as "iambic," "dactylic," etc., all somewhat confusingly named for Greek meters in a totally different system.

3. *Pure syllabic*—the basic system of modern French and Japanese, to cite two kinds of poetry that have used it for centuries; it has been used in English only in the last fifty years or so.

4. So-called *free verse*, of which there are many varieties, developed mostly in the twentieth century.

5. *Quantitative verse* which, save for some grotesque and failed examples, cannot occur in English, but which was the basis of Greek prosody and, later on, of Latin.

Since accentual-syllabism has been so dominant, and so important, during the course of the poetic history of the English language, we will start with it.

Accentual-syllabic verse is built up of pairs or triads of syllables, alternating or otherwise grouping stressed and unstressed ones. Syllables usually keep their word accent, or the accent they would have in phrases in normal speech. *Iambic pentameter*, a line pattern made up of five syllable pairs with the first syllable unstressed, can be illustrated by a line which most perfectly conforms to the pattern itself:

About about about about about

or this:

A boat, a boat, a boat, a boat, a boat

(for a monosyllable, with its preceding article, is accented like a word of two syllables). But actual lines of iambic pentameter, because they can't simply repeat identical pairs of syllables, have individual and particular rhythms which depart from the metrical pattern slightly. It is in this variation that the sound of poetry lives. For example, a simple variation of our first example—one that has become a standard pattern in itself—is actually a reversal of stressed and unstressed syllables in the first pair: ˙

> *Al*most "a*bout* a*bout* a*bout* a*bout*"

or in the second as well:

> *Near*ly *al*most "a*bout* a*bout* a*bout*"

But there are ways of departing that seem to obscure the pattern so that they can no longer be considered variations from it:

> *Al*most the *sound* of the *line* of "*about*"s

What we hear is a rhythm of four beats, not five, and the unstressed syllables are grouped into triads of *dum* de de, *dum* de de (called dactyls), even though there are, in fact, ten syllables in the lines.

Most interesting with regard to poetry are the variations—and almost every line of poetry exhibits them—that lie between these extremes. Any poem will be cast in one metrical form or another, and after we read three or more lines it will be obvious which of two patterns even the most ambiguous line is a variation of. Frequently, richness and significance of sound depend upon our ear hesitating for a while between patterns; but there is real ambiguity only at the start of a poem. An extreme case is the opening of one of Keats's sonnets:

> How many bards gild the lapses of time

We might think that a matching line would be:

> Read this as dactyls and then it will rhyme

like the one we made up before. But in fact, the sonnet continues in iambic pentameter, and we realize that we had a wildly variant first line instead of a more patterned one. But a better example, also by Keats, can be seen in the second line of his "Ode on a Grecian Urn":

> Thou fóster-chíld of sílence and slów tíme

Here, although only the fourth pair has its order reversed, the line nevertheless resounds with other possibilities. Thus,

> Thou fóster-child of sílence and slów tíme
> Accéntually póunding to só míme
> An ántiquated rhýthm which had nó rhýme.

But the phrase "slow time" resolves itself in the poem because "time" rhymes there only with the monosyllable "rhyme" two lines below (there's no "slow"/ "so" chiming, as in our example). When we *scan* a line of poetry, or mark the prominent syllables, we are really showing what its actual rhythm is, and then, by putting this rhythm in alignment with adjacent ones in the poem or stanza of the poem, deciding what their common pattern is. Thus, every line is at once unique and has family resemblances, usually very strong, to its companions in any one poem.

Accentual-syllabic verse is traditionally discussed as sequences of *feet*; and although the terminology is misleading, you can remember that:

> A foot | is just | a group | of syl- | lables:
> Trochees | (like these), | iambs, | spondees, | paired, while
> Dactyls and | anapests | always are | triads of | syllables.

An iamb is a pair with a stress on the second syllable (as in "about"):

> Iambic meter runs along like this:
> *Pentameters* will have five syllables
> More strongly stressed than other ones nearby—
> Ten syllables all told, perhaps eleven.

But

> *Trochees* simply tumble on and
> Start with downbeats just like this one
> (Sorry, "iamb" is trochaic).
>
> ★
>
> *"Dactyl"* means | "finger" in | Greek, and a | foot that was
> | made up of | one long
> Syllable followed by two, like the joints in a finger was used
> for
> Lines made of six, just like these, in the epics of Homer and
> Virgil,
> Save that in English we substitute downbeats and upbeats
> for long-short.*
>
> ★
>
> In an *an* | *apest* up | beats start out | in reverse
> Of the dactyl's persuasion but end up no worse.
> (Yes, the anapest's name is dactylic—a curse?)
>
> ★
>
> Slow *spondees* are two heavy stressed downbeats
> They stand shoulder to strong shoulder this way.

*For more on this, see pages 34–36.

We can even observe the echoes of such accentual "feet" in natural speech:

> So names such as "John Smith" seem spondees.
> (Names of places, such as "Main Street"?*
> These are merely good old trochees.)

It will be clear by now that different kinds of accentual-syllabic line will "interpret" a stress-pattern of natural speech in different ways. Disyllabic words are stressed either one way or another, and pairs of words that differ by virtue of stress alone will have to play different metrical roles:

> These lines can show you where the accent went,
> But with their content I'm not yet content.

And trisyllables, for example, can submit to two readings. We would say that "typewriter" is normally dactyllic-sounding, and placing it in a dactyllic line elicits this character.

> Listen, my typewriter clatters in dactyls along with my
>   prose!

But "typewriter" is a compound word, once hyphenated ("type-writer") before constant use in speech had silenced the second stress; that ghost of accent can be summoned up:

> My typewriter in verse divides its time
> Between iamb and trochee. (Now I'll rhyme.)

Clearly, a little phrase like "open it" will work like a dactyllic single word, just as "of the best" will work like an anapestic one. It will be apparent, also, that accentual-syllabic verse can make much of the variations of stress that occur when we are logically con-

*(But a town's "main street" 's spondaic.)

trasting two words or phrases which differ by reason of their unstressed syllable. "A book" is an iamb; so is "the book"; but what we write as "*the* book" (and pronounce as something like "thee book") promotes the unstressed syllable, in emphatic contrast, to something having more of the power of "this book" or "that book." Thus we might, iambically,

> Observe the whore outside the store.

But if we mean to single out the allegorical figure of Revelation 17 then she may become trochaic, when

> Babylon we mean here—*the* whore
> (Not some hooker by the seashore).

When the older terminology of "foot" for "syllable pair" or "triad" is used, line length is described in terms of number of feet, as for example *di*meter, *tri*meter:

> If she should write
> Some verse tonight
> This dimeter
> Would limit her.

But:

> Iambic trimeter
> Is rather easier.

And:

> *Tetrameter* allows more space
> For thoughts to seat themselves with grace.

Now:

> Here is *pentameter*, the line of five
> That English poetry still keeps alive;

In other centuries it was official.
Now, different kinds of verse make it seem special.

★

Six downbeats in a line that has twelve syllables
Make up the *alexandrine*, which, as you can hear,
Tends to fall into halves—one question, one reply.

The break that you heard in the last line is called
caesura. Here it is at work in rhymed pairs of lines
called *couplets:*

In couplets, one line often makes a point
Which hinges on its bending, like a joint;
The sentence makes that line break into two.
Here's a *caesura:* see what it can do.
(And here's a gentler one, whose pause, more slight,
Waves its two hands, and makes what's left sound right.)

Two even longer measured lines:

Fourteeners, cut from *ballad stanzas*, don't seem right for song:
Their measure rumbles on like this for just a bit too long.

and, used by early Elizabethans,

A *poulter's measure* (like a baker's dozen) cut
One foot off a fourteener couplet, ended in a rut.

Let us now consider groupings of lines, by rhyme
or other means, remembering first that

A line can be *end-stopped*, just like this one,
Or it can show *enjambment*, just like this
One, where the sense straddles two lines: you feel
As if from shore you'd stepped into a boat;

and remembering secondly that there is a unique
case, outside of line-groups. The one-line poem (in
Greek, a *monostich*) is almost always really a couplet,

an epigram formed by the title and the line itself, as in

A ONE-LINE POEM

The universe

First, then, *blank verse:*

Iambic five-beat lines are labeled *blank*
Verse (with sometimes a foot or two reversed,
Or one more syllable—"feminine ending").
Blank verse can be extremely flexible:
It ticks and tocks the time with even feet
(Or sometimes, cleverly, can end limping).*
Shakespeare and others of his day explored
Blank verse in stage plays, both in regular
And rather uneven and more rough-hewn forms.
Occasionally, rhyming couplets sound
Out at scenes' endings, gongs to end the round.
Milton did other things: he made it more
Heroic than dramatic: although blind
He turned its structure into something half
Heard, half seen, as when a *chiasm*†
(Words, phrases, sounds or parts of speech arranged
In mirroring) occurs in *Paradise*
Lost (he often *enjambs* this way) we see
Half a line that, reflecting its line-half,
Cannot sit still to be regarded like
A well-made picture or inscription, but
Rushes ahead as sentences do, not like
Visual melody in a well-shaped line.
But back again to what blank verse can do:
In time of old, inversions it contained
Of syntax, and Wordsworth and Tennyson
More delicately such arrangements made.
But Browning and more lately Robert Frost
Made their blank verse seem natural again,
The kind of sound our sentences would make

*(Pentameters like this are called *scazons.*)
†And see page 49.

> If only we could leave them to themselves—
> The road our way of talking always takes,
> Not, like a foul line or state boundary,
> An artificially drawn line at all.

But:

> The old fourteener William Blake found to his liking more
> Than old "heroic" verse, pentameters, which must have
>   seemed
> Far too *official* for him; so, like Milton with his ten
> Syllables, Blake pushed ahead with the seven stresses he
>   heard beneath
> The even fourteeners sanctified for him by balladry
> (For two rhyming fourteeners can / be written out, you see,
> In just a single ballad stan- / za, rhymed *abab*)
> And common hymnody, and Chapman's *Iliad*, and all
> Popular rhyming forms eschewed by Alexander Pope.
> Blake, in *Jerusalem* and *Milton*, twisted the seven-beat line
> With terrible vatic force, & claimed that he wrote in three
>   different keys,
> "Terrific," "Mild & gentle," and "Prosaic"; yet it remains
> Hard to distinguish their tones, as it were, from rhythmic
>   patterns alone.

Before we move into groupings made by rhyme, let us consider the ways in which syllables themselves can reach through, or across, lines. They can *alliterate:*

> *Alliteration* lightly links
> Stressed syllables with common consonants.

And they can, without actually rhyming, exhibit *assonance:*

> *Assonance* is the spirit of a rhyme,
> A common vowel, hovering like a sigh
> After its consonantal body dies.

We should also remember the following, about rhyme itself:

The weakest way in which two words can chime
Is with the most expected kind of rhyme—
(If it's the only rhyme that you can write,
A homonym will never sound quite right.)
A rhyme is stronger when the final words
Seem less alike than pairs of mated birds.
When meaning makes a gap which sound can span, it's
As if the rhyme words came from different planets;
Or when a final verb, perhaps, will reach
Out to rhyme with some different part of speech;
Or when a word spelled in one way, like "off,"
Rhymes strictly, with a sort of visual cough
Of surprise; or when a common word like "love"
Which rhymed in Shakespeare's time with "move" and
    "prove"
Ends up today a sight-rhyme, as above.
Some rhymes can trip you as you move along:
Their lines can seem as smooth as they are strong.
Like a typewriter's final, right-hand bell,
A rhyme can stop a line, or it can tell
The sentence to go on and do its best
Till, at the next line's end, it comes to rest.
And if the tone shows signs of letting up, let
There be a cute rhyme for a final couplet.
(A serious effect is often killable
By rhyming with *too* much more than one syllable.)

Internal rhymes can claim a word or name
And make two words mean something of the same:
Thus *spring* can *jingle* with its *singing* birds,
Or *summer hum* with two resounding words;
The red *robes* of *October's* garish ball
Make *fall recall* that dropping leaves are all
We hear; the hard, dry stint of winter lasts
Through blizzards and through *slow* and *snowy* blasts,
Until lengthening sunlight hours will bring
Round in a *ring*like way again, the *spring*.

One of the most important groupings of lines we
have had in English, particularly in the seventeenth
through the nineteenth centuries, has been the English couplet, paired rhymed iambic pentameter:

Heroic couplets, classical and cold,
Can make new matters smack of something old
And something borrowed (like a wedding, true,
But this comparison stops short of "blue"
Yet points out how the marriage of two lines ⎫
Brings forth long children as their length combines ⎬
—And sometimes triplets help to vary the designs). ⎭
This verse was called "heroic" for the way
It seemed equivalent, in Jonson's day—
The seventeenth century—to Homer's long
Unrhymed hexameters, and Virgil's song.
With Alexander Pope, we have so pure a
Way of arranging these, that a *caesura*
Makes this line pause, makes that one slowly wend
Its way to join its partner in the end.
An *end-stopped* line is one—as you'll have guessed—
Whose syntax comes, just at its end, to rest.
But when the walking sentence needs to keep
On going, the *enjambment* makes a leap
Across a line-end (here, a rhyming close).
—Milton, in his blank verse, makes use of those:
His long, dependent clauses are enjambed.
A somewhat sharp effect, as well, is damned
Easy—when, reading on, the reader learns
The maze of verse can have its sudden turns
And twists—but couplets take your hand, and then
Lead you back into end-stopped rhyme again.

Of course,

Couplets can be of any length,
And shorter size gives greater strength
Sometimes—but sometimes, willy-nilly,
Four-beat couplets sound quite silly.
(Some lines really should stay single:
Feminine rhymes can make them jingle.)

These *anapestic tetrameter* couplets, by the way, were used widely in the late eighteenth and the early nineteenth centuries; they can seem either active or passively elegiac:

There are rhythms like this that you'll frequently meet:
They resound with the pounding of regular feet,
And their anapests carry a narrative load
(The hoofbeats of horses, of course, on the road).

★

But they lie by the side of a whispering stream
Flowing slowly as time, gliding by in a dream.

Now, then:

Tercets are groups of three; they are a band
—Playful, like couplets that get out of hand—
Of lines that fly far, then come back to land.

★

A *quatrain* has four lines
    As one can plainly see:
One of its strict designs
    Comes rhymed *abab*.

★

Another way of rhyme can come
    From *abba* (middle two
    Lines holding hands as lovers do)
In Tennyson's *In Memoriam*.

★

After the heyday of such rhyme's renown,
After the weariness of World War I,
Modern poets built in a sad letdown
By rhyming quatrains thus: *abax*.

★

The *ballad stanza*'s four short lines
    Are very often heard;
The second and the fourth lines rhyme
    But not the first and third.

★

The ballad stanza in a hymn
    Waits on the music's pleasure,

And hymnals (hardly out of whim)
  Call it the "common measure."

★

(The attic heart's—theology
Reformed—this hymnal scheme
In Emily Dickinson's—Amherst—house
And slanted—away—the rhyme.)

★

"Long measure" in the hymnody
Means even quatrains just like this,
Whose music sets the spirit free,
Doctrine dissolved in choral bliss.

★

Translating Omar Khayyam's *Rubaiyat*,
Edward Fitzgerald, it would seem, forgot
To rhyme the third line with the other ones.
(The last line underscored its lonely lot.)

He didn't, really: I meant no aspersion.
His gloomy quatrains were an English version
Of just that rhyme scheme (and God knows what else)
He found in the original in Persian.

★

Lord Byron, seeking out a verse to dally in
  While roaming through *Don Juan*, came to see
The point of imitating the Italian
  Poets back in the sixteenth century:
Don Juan's stanza, jumping like a stallion
  Over its disyllabic rhymes, and free
Of too much room to roam in, came to seem a
Verse pattern all its own *(ottava rima).*

★

One more famous stanza should be described here;
It can come rhymed, unrhymed, or what you will, at
Least in English; it's named for the great Greek poet
  Passionate Sappho . . .

Sapphics: four-line stanzas whose first three lines are

Heard—in our hard English at least—as heartbeats,
Then, in one more touch of a final short line,
    Tenderly ending.

★

Rhyme royal is a stanza form of seven
Pentameters, which Chaucer filled with scenes
From *Troilus and Criseyde* and with heaven-
Sent birdsong in the *Parlement*, its means
More limited than are *The Faerie Queene*'s.
"Royal"?—from a poem by Scotland's first King James.
(Some scholars differ: so it is with names.)

★

A true *Spenserian stanza* wakes up well
With what will seem a quatrain first; in time
The third line rings its "a" rhyme like a bell,
The fourth, its "b" resounding like a dime
In a pay telephone—this paradigm
Demonstrating the kind of interlocking
Of quatrains doubling back on the same rhyme
Ends in an alexandrine, gently rocking
The stanza back to sleep, lest the close be too shocking.

(And so the questions that the last lines ask
The alexandrine answers, as a pleasant task.)

There is a famous way of interlocking tercets:

The unrhymed middle line, in the tight schema
Of tercets spinning out a lengthy text
(Dante gave us this form, called *terza rima*),

Rhymes, after all, with the start of the next
Tercet, then helps set up a new unrhyme
That, sure of foot and not at all perplexed,

Walks across blank space, as it did last time.
(A couplet ends this little paradigm.)

In general,

A *stanza* in Italian means "a room";
    In verse, it needn't keep to square

Corners, as of some dismal tomb,
  But wanders anywhere:
Some stanzas can be built of many lines
    Of differing length;
  Their variation then combines
    With rhymes to give it strength.
      Along the way
      Short lines can play,
  And, at the end, a longer and more solemn
Line extends below, a broad base for a column.

Sonnets can be of two general sorts—the so-called
Elizabethan form, with three quatrains and a couplet,
or the Italian kind, with an *octave* rhymed *abba abba*
and a *sestet* of various groupings of *cde*. Here are the
two types:

The kind of *sonnet* form that Shakespeare wrote
—A poem of Love, or Time, in fourteen lines
Rhymed the way these are, clear, easy to quote—
Channels strong feelings into deep designs.
Three *quatrains* neatly fitting limb to joint,
Their lines cut with the sharpness of a prism,
Flash out in colors as they make their point
In what logicians call a syllogism—
(*If A, and B, then C*)—and so it goes.
Unless the final quatrain starts out "But"
Or "Nevertheless," these groups of lines dispose
Themselves in reasoned sections, tightly shut.
    The final couplet's tight and terse and tends
    To sum up neatly how the sonnet ends.
★

Milton and Wordsworth made the sonnet sound
Again in a new way; not with the sighs
Of witty passion, where fierce reason lies
Entombed in end-stopped lines, or tightly bound
In chains of quatrain: more like something found
Than built—a smooth stone on a sandy rise,
A drop of dew secreted from the sky's
Altitude, unpartitioned, whole and round.

The *octave*'s over; now, gently defying
Its opening tone, the *sestet* then recalls
Old rhythms and old thoughts, enjambed, half-heard
As verses in themselves. The final word,
Five lines away from what it rhymes with, falls
Off into silence, like an echo dying.

There have been other slight variations on fixed
sonnet patterns, some of them—like film stars that
are shaped by, and shape, their roles—informing and
being blooded, at once, by major poetic occasions.

Another sonnet form, though hardly shocking,
Presents us with three quatrains, like the rest,
But runs the rhymes into an interlocking
Pattern that asks the poet for his best
As each new quatrain puts him to the test
(Or, her, as the case often is), by way
Of having at such moments to divest
Himself of rhyme-words waiting, an array
Of crowded sounds he'd treasured up all day.
No need for noisy ingenuities,
Though; one needs but two rhymes on *d* and *a*
(-*Ay's* the last *c*-rhyme: there were four of these.)
Such lines that intertwine, like cooked spaghetti,
Were used by Spenser in his *Amoretti*.

Milton once composed a "tailed sonnet" of twenty
lines:

After the sestet of a sonnet, six
More lines are added, playing more than tricks,
          And thereupon we fix
Two shorter, caudal lines that cannot fail
To drag it out; we hammer on a nail
          And thereby hangs a tail,
But I'll not tell it now; instead, we'll call
It quits, and close in couplet after all.

★

And as for *Modern Love*, George Meredith,
Who brooded most ironically upon it,

Used an extended variant of the sonnet
To do his sad demystifying with
(Of Eros, and of Hymen, God of marriage,
Who, to the sound of flagrant, wailing willows
And low reproaches muttered on the pillows,
Descended in an armor-plated carriage).
Behold the form that disillusion takes!
The *abba* quatrain of the old
Italian mode, its stories oversold,
Goes rambling past the point at which it breaks
Off, and the sestet finishes. Unsweet
Sixteen, this sonnet-pattern might be named,
Ending in embers where once passion flamed,
Sadder and wiser and not half so neat.

★

One final recent variant of sonnet form works
Its way purely syllabically,* in unrhymed lines
Of thirteen syllables, and then squares these off with one
Less line in the whole poem—a thirteener-by-thirteen.
But hidden in its unstressed trees there can lurk rhyming
Lines like these (for instance); as in all syllabic verse
Moments of audible accent pass across the face
Of meditation, summoning old themes to the fair
Courtroom of revision, flowing into parts of eight
And five lines, seven and six, or unrhymed quatrains,
Or triplets, that like this one with unaligned accents
Never jingles in its threes or imbecilities.
Then the final line, uncoupled, can have the last word.

Before we examine some of the more extended
traditional forms, we might consider the working of
other systems of verse listed on page 5. *Pure accentual*
meter, which we all know from the first oral poetry
we hear—nursery rhymes and so forth—measures
stressed syllables only:

In ac*cen*tual *me*ter it *does*n't *mat*ter
*Whe*ther each *line* is *thin* or *fat*ter;

*See the next page for why this line doesn't seem to scan.

What you *hear* (this *mat*ters *more*)
Is *one, two, three, four.*

In medieval times,

The oldest English   accented meter
Of four, unfailing,   fairly audible
Strongly struck   stresses seldom
Attended to anything   other than
Definite downbeats: how many dim
Unstressed upbeats   in any line
Mattered not much;   motion was measured
With low leaps   of alliteration
Handily harping on   heavy accents
(Echoing equally   all vowels,
Consonant cousins   coming together).

The spirit of purely accentual verse was summoned up by an eminent Victorian:

Sprung rhythm is modern accentual, counting the downbeats.
Instead of pentameter, Gerard Manley Hopkins' verse
Rains down in no shower, but as the sound of a town beats
Down on the ear in a queer-clear way; his terse
Compound words, noun-to-noun-tethered, togethered with
    strange
Wordings (not absurdings) roamed his rhythms' range.

★

Verse called *skeltonic*
Is not cacophonic;
Jiggly and jumpy,
Loose, somewhat lumpy,
Pleasing or prating,
Graceful or grating,
It's always elating,
Often alliterating
Short lines, and neat,
With double downbeat
(Don't scan them in "feet")
Whose rhymes repeat
Forever—no feat

When the measure's meet—
Mixed in with lines like these,
Clearly accented in threes,
Named for John Skelton,
Scholar-poet who dwelt in
Diss, Norfolk, and then
Paraded his pen
To great reknown
In London town
(Born, as far as we know,
In 1460 or so,
Did this world resign
In 1529).
Such lines, so crammed,
Would be doubly damned
Before being enjambed,
Their line-endings lopped,
Criminally cropped
With syntax dropped.
They are all end-stopped.
A skillful skeltonic
May be macaronic.*

Pure syllabic verse—sometimes called "isosyllabic"—
is an importation into English from other languages.
Its lines can be of any length.

Whereas iambic verse will let you hear
Five downbeats, countable inside your ear,

*(In Latin, *id est*,
A magpie's nest
Of languages various,
Stern or hilarious:
Deutsch and *Français*
Together can play
In this wanton way
With *la lingua Italiana*,
Hoy y mañana
When readers understand 'em:
Quod erat demonstrandum.)

Lines made up of ten syllables purely
Without any arrangement of downbeats
Will not seem to be in any meter,
And rhyme becomes something this form defeats.

Thus decasyllabic verse in French or
Japanese, unaccented, will sound like
Something strange to English ears, which still lust
For downbeats, drumbeats (*something*) in a line,
A last syllable at least, stressed, which hits
The nail of a rhyme-word: thus rhyme limits,—
If we are to *hear* it (not as above)—
Pure syllabic wandering. W.
H. Auden and Marianne Moore both wrote
In syllabic meter like this, which can
Always regain a pure *iambic* voice
By sorting out the accents in its words
In any line, or rush into hiding
Again, in caves of accentless shadow.

★

And stanzas made
up of lines
of varying length
like this one—
with four, three, five, three, six
syllables, and then one of eight—

are quite clearly
of the same
form as each other;
but only
the counting eye can tell:
You use your fingers, not your ear.

One conventional pure syllabic form, borrowed from
Japanese poetry, has been popular in English verse
for over twenty years:

Haiku, with seven
Syllables in between two
Shorter lines of five,

Gently—like cherry
Blossoms in a breeze—allude
To just one season

Sometimes: they are a
Peculiarly Japanese
Form of epigram.

In them, brevity
Lights up with significance
Like a firefly.

The *cinquain* in older French verse was any kind of
five-line stanza. But in English,

Cinquains
Have lines of four
Syllables, six, and eight,
Ending, as starting, with a line
Of two;

But when
Iambs align
To the trained ear these seem
To form a line of twelve, and then
Of ten.

Cinquains
In English verse
Were devised by a bard
Whose name (alas!) was Adelaide
Crapsey.

Accentual-syllabic, pure accentual, and pure syllabic verse all count or measure units—either syllables or just accented ones or both—to determine a
line. But various kinds of unmeasured verse exist,
and have for ages. The most influential of these is
the verse form of the Hebrew Bible, as it was trans-
lated into English and thereby resonated throughout
the language in quotation, allusion, and echo.

The verse of the Hebrew Bible is strange; the meter of Psalms
  and Proverbs perplexes.
It is not a matter of number, no counting of beats or syllables.
Its song is a music of matching, its rhythm a kind of
  paralleling.
One half-line makes an assertion; the other part paraphrases
  it; sometimes a third part will vary it.
An abstract statement meets with its example, yes, the way
  a wind runs through the tree's moving leaves.
One river's water is heard on another's shore; so did this
  Hebrew verse form carry across into English.

Modern *free verse*, influenced by the inventiveness
of Walt Whitman in English (and Arthur Rimbaud
among others in French), can be of many sorts; since
a line may be determined in almost any way, and
since lines may be grouped on the page in any fash-
ion, it is the mode of variation itself which is sig-
nificant. Here are examples of a number of different
types:

Free verse is never totally "free":
It can occur in many forms,
All of them having in common one principle—
Nothing is necessarily counted or measured
(Remember biblical verse—see above).
One form—this one—makes each line a grammatical unit.
This can be a clause
Which has a subject and a predicate,
Or a phrase
Of prepositional type.
The in-and-out variation of line length
Can provide a visual "music" of its own, a rhythm
That, sometimes, indented lines
                              like diagrammed sentences
Can reinforce.
Our eye—and perhaps in a funny, metaphorical way, our
  breath itself—
Can be dragged far out, by some rather longer line, across
  the page,

Then made to trip
On short lines:
The effect is often wry.
Yet such verse often tends
To fall very flat.

★

Another kind of free verse can play a
sort of rhythmic tune at the end
of lines, moving back and forth from those that stop
to those that are enjambed as
sharply as that first one.
Aside from the rhythmic tension
Of varying the ebb and flow of
sense along the lines, of making them seem
more (like this one), or less, like measured lines
(like this
one), this sort of free verse can direct our attention
as well as any iambic line, for
instance, to what our language is made up of:
it can break up compound words at line-ends, sometimes
    wittily,
(like someone talking in winter of a whole hiber-
nation of bears)
like tripping hurriedly over what, when you look
down, turns out to have been a grave
stone.

★

Some free verse is arranged in various
graphic patterns like this that suggest
the barely-seen but silent ghost of a
        classical verse form

like a fragment of Sapphic . . .

★

Free verse can, like a shrewd smuggler, contain more
Measured kinds of line, hidden
inside its own more random-seeming
ones; and when a bit of song
comes, blown in on a kind of wind, it will move

across my country
'tis of thee, sweet land
of liberty,
of thee
I sing—the accented verses get cut up
by line breaks that reveal something about them we'd
never seen before: it's a little
like putting a contour map over a street plan
(Customs inspector: are you
trained to hear heroic couplets beating
on the ear if they are hidden in the linings
of free verse, as in the case of these above?)

★

Free verse can build up various
stanzalike units without
rhyme or measured line length to hold
them together, but the power of blank

space between them marks out their rhythms
as surely as the timing of some iambic clock
but, of course, silently: the
ear alone can't tell where they end.

★

Free verse can be a way of making lines that surge
With a power of rhythmic motion, pulsing and oceanic, then
Break, as if a jetty of tumbled boulders had thrust a long
    finger out into the
Surf, making the rumble of water irregular, keeping
The lines from becoming too
Metrical, marked with the yardstick
Of dactyls.

★

A milder kind
of *vers libre*
as it was called
earlier in this century

Hardly ever enjambed its lines,
but used the linear unit

and even stanzalike
gatherings of lines
as a delicate way of controlling,
of slowing
the pace of the reading eye
or speeding it up across the page again.

It could single out
words
and hang them in lines all their own
Like sole blossoms on branches,
made more precious
by their loneliness.

★

And to be able to wander, free
                        (in a wide field, as it were)
verse can amble about
        on a kind of nature walk
                    the lines following no
            usual path, for
            then the poem might seem
            to have wandered into
        another kind of meter's backyard
                                    but

                                        sometimes
                        seeming
                            to map out the syntax,
                                        sometimes
                    seeming to do almost the
                                opposite,
        this kind of meandering verse can
                                    even

oddly

                come upon a flower
                of familiar rhythm
                                a sight for sore
        ears, or encounter
                        a bit later
on,
            once again a patch of

```
            trochees growing somewhere
                                        (like an old song)
                                                       and
            take one by the
                          stem
                 and
                          break
                 it
                     off
```

And, finally, a unique kind of rhymed free verse, but of a sort that really can only be considered as antiverse:

> Because light verse makes meter sound easy,
> And because saying something just for the rhyme is inept and, well, cheesy,
> Even when you spice up rhyme
> With jokes about sagely beating thyme
> (Although *that* line is more compelling
> As a joke about English spelling)
> A famous comic writer whose name follows developed a deliberate and highly skilled method of writing lines that didn't even try to scan so that the general effect was of a metrical hash:
> Ogden Nash.

One formal aberration has reappeared from time to time, in the Hellenistic age, in the Renaissance, and in modern decades. The so-called *pattern-poem* (or "shaped verse" or, as Guillaume Apollinaire referred to his own French exercises, "calligrammes") is composed in, or typographically arranged in, shapes of images of objects or abstract forms, from some aspect of which the poem's "subject" or occasion will arise. An instance of a sort that is composed directly, rather than arranged by a compositor after being written, is this:

```
                        This is
                  a macrodot-shaped
                 poem by which we mean
               not   merely   a   disc   or   an
               emblematic    circle    which    a
             text    so    figured    might    claim
             meant   sun   moon   world   eternity
             or   perfection   No   Just   a   blown
              up  dot  in  lines  of  7  up  to  29
               letters   Past   the   middle   the
                lines  of  type  get  shorter
                 and  move  faster  but  all
                  adding up to too much
                    fuss about making
                       a point.
```

A Renaissance version of an ancient adage char-
acterized poetry as speaking picture, and art as mute
poesy. Poetic form can try to avoid the ear by hiding
more and more in its visual areas. Pattern-poems are
the most extreme instance of this that we have seen.
But *concrete poetry*, a development in graphic art of
the past thirty years or so (but developing from ty-
pographical experimentation going back to Mallarmé
in the later nineteenth century) depends upon unique
drawn, printed, or assembled representations of patterned inscription, punning rebus, etc. It most often
cannot be read aloud the way all verse can (no matter
how framed or commented-upon by visual aspects
of its meter). Consider, for example, a little concrete
poem I might call "On Touching Sunsets":

```
                      c  c
                      u  u
```

The reading ("To see's to use"—2c's, 2u's) makes a
crepuscular epigram about the use and misuse of
nature. This case is more translatable into speech
than most; the self-descriptive example prepared for

this volume is, alas, too heavy for these light pages.
I include not it, but instructions for realizing it; having followed same, readers will also realize why I
have not burdened them with the actual example.
Here is the account of it:

> "Concrete Poem" by John Hollander is to be found in the
> keeping of the Yale University Press. It *is* (rather than, as
> in the case of real verse or prose, being "inscribed upon,"
> "written across," etc.) a concrete slab, 2' × 2', heavily
> scuffed, scarred, rubbed—its surface texture very rough,
> cobwebbed, and active. Discernible upon it are inscribed
> words, disposed as represented below. The poem's surface
> is such that the last three letters of the word "texture" recede
> into its texture. Needless to say, the illustration given here
> *is not, nor can ever be,* the concrete poem. And just as well.

Repetition is a powerful and diversified element of formal structures. It is also a very ancient one: primitive work songs, or prayers, or danced rituals, all involved a solo singer or leader, who would chant new and developing material, and a chorus, who would repeat some shorter element over and over as a kind of punctuation of the new material. Before considering refrains and other modern kinds of repetition, we should distinguish between this primitive but continuing kind of solo-chorus structure and the vastly complex pattern of the Greek choral ode, whether used in tragedy or in public ceremonies. Although Greek verse, as we shall see shortly, used a system of syllable lengths rather than stressed accents, you can see what a typical pattern was like:

> The *choral ode*
> in ancient Greece was more
> than just a verse form: for each section
> (like this one), called a *strophe*
> was sung—not recited—and danced,
> and the dancers were singers.
> These words to their music moved
> with the dancers in one direction,
> then finished their pattern
> at the end of part of what they had to say.
>
> The second part
> of every section then
> would have the same tune, the same rhythm,
> the strophe had, and therefore
> the whole *antistrophe* would move
> with a parallel motion.
> (This matching of verse to verse
> is referred to as *contrafactum*.)
> The dancers moved back then
> as they sang with those same steps the other way.
>
> And then a last, unmatching section
> called an *epode*, or standing,

> followed the strophe (or "turn")
> and the antistrophe (or "counterturn")
> and, rather more simply, perhaps,
> completed the *triad* or section
> of which there could be one or several.

But "ode" has another sense, that of a neoclassical lyric in some accentual-syllabic verse scheme perhaps adapted from Horace. So:

> Pindar's public, grand to-do
> Andrew Marvell contracted to
>   The semi-private mode
>   Of his "Horatian Ode";
>
> The rhyming first and second lines
> Of this compactest of designs
>   Are followed everywhere
>   By a much shorter pair.

A consideration of the whole matter of neoclassical form might be prefaced by some brief observations about *quantitative verse*. Greek meter was based on syllabic quantities, rather than contrasting stresses; one long syllable (so determined by the length of the vowel, and by a few positional rules) was set equal to two short ones, like half notes and quarter notes in musical notation. A *foot* in quantitative scansion was like a musical measure: a dactyl was like one of 4/4 time that could have either two half notes, or a half and two quarters (that is, a dactyl, $-\cup\cup$, or a spondee, $-\,-$). In Latin, where spoken words tended to have a stress accent on the penultimate syllable, following the Greek rules which observed no word accent (but instead placed a musical down-beat on the long syllable in a foot or bar) made for some phonetic confusion.

We are concerned only with English verse, how-
ever, and its attempts to "imitate" classical meters.
Even more than in Latin, stress dominates English
grammar and syntax, and in order to set up classical
verse forms in English, some kind of metaphoric
version of them had to be framed before poets of the
Renaissance and later, yearning for the voice of an-
tiquity, could imitate them in stressed, romance-
trained English.

One early solution was to assign to English vowels
the length of the analogous ones in Greek or Latin,
and count any syllable "long" that was followed by
two adjacent consonants. Audible stress-accent was
discounted. And thus, in these putatively "quantitative" dactyllic hexameters,

> Āll sūch sўllăblĕs arrāng'd ĭn thē clāssĭcăl ōrdĕr
> Cān't bĕ aūdĭblĕ tŏ Ēnglīsh ēars thăt ăre tūn'd tŏ ăn āccĕnt
> Mārk'd bў ă pāttĕrn ōf strēss, nōt bў ă quāntĭtătĭve crāwl.

These lines "scan" only if we show that the pattern
of "long" and "short" syllables falls into the classical
"feet," or musical measures. The inaudibility of these
quantities in any language that had stressed syllables
was a factor in Latin verse; stressed syllables could
either be placed in the positions of long ones, or not.
In the former case, they are called (using the terminology of one modern scholar)

> hómodyne | dáctyls

In the latter case, heterodyne. Stressed syllables

> Sŏúndĕd ŏut | eách līne's | énd ĭn | Vírgĭl's | tērmĭnăl | āccēnts.

Later on, classical adaptations tried less to be so

literal, and replaced the classical feet, or measures
of longs and shorts, with paired or trined stressed
and unstressed syllables. Thus, the classical iamb,
or short-long, became the English one, or da-*dum*.
Some eighteenth-century German poets wrote in accentual elegiac couplets,

> First a hexameter stretching its dactyls across to a cadence,
>   Then the pentameter line follows and falls to a close.

Accentual versions of stanza forms also occur. We
have come across the accentual sapphic already (page
17). Another strophic type, named for the Greek poet
Alcaeus, was adapted by Horace and then imitated
from him:

> This tight alcaic stanza begins with a
> Matched pair of longer lines that are followed by
>   Two shorter ones, indented *this* way,
>   Making the meter declaim in English.
>
> So ghosts of ancient structures survive even
> Slow ruin: alcaics somehow outlasted the
>   Greek poets, Roman ones, and Germans
>   (Hölderlin, Klopstock) who made it modern.

Ultimately, modern quatrain forms of two longer,
followed by two shorter, lines are all implicit versions
of this stanza (see the so-called Horatian Ode stanza
of Andrew Marvell, page 34).

> One more version of "classical" stressed meter
> Called *hendecasyllabics* (which is Greek for
> Having syllables numbering eleven)
> Starts right out with a downbeat, always ending
> Feminine, with a kind of hesitation
> Heard just after the pair of syllables (the
> Fourth and fifth ones) which give the line its pattern.

> Three stressed syllables sometimes open up this
> Line, which, used in Latin by carping Martial
> (Even more by fantastical Catullus)
> Still holds on to its old, upbraiding cadence.

And this is as good a place as any for two kinds of tricky device, both neoclassical in origin:

> *A*crostic verse ("end of the line," in Greek)
> *C*onceals, in a linguistic hide-and-seek,
> *R*eadable messages, gems sunk in fetters—
> *O*nly read down the lines' initial letters.
> *S*ometimes a loved name here encoded lies:
> *T*his instance names itself (surprise, surprise!)
> *I*ndeed, these final lines, demure and winning,
> *C*onfirm the guess you'd made near the beginning.

Descending from Alexandrian times through the eighteenth century, a witty device known usually as *echo verse* would simulate the syllabic repetitions and truncations of natural echoes for satiric effect:

> Echo will have it that each line's last word
> (ECHO:)   *Erred.*
> Echo will chop down words like "fantasize"
> (ECHO:)   *To size.*
> Out of what stuff is Echo's wit then spun?
> (ECHO:)   *Pun.*
> Can English have a full, Italian echo?
> (ECHO:)   *Ecco!*

We shall now return to the matter of repetition. One kind of medieval European dance song was called a *carol*, or ring dance. In a carol, the leader would sing the stanzas, and the dancers the refrain or *burden:*

> The dancers flutter about
> Like a circle of fluttering birds,
> The leader stands in place

And remembers many more words.
> *Birdily, birdily bright*
> *Their burden is very light.*

The dancers circle about
Like a ring around the moon,
Their singing a kind of dance,
Their language a kind of tune.
> *Birdily, birdily bright*
> *Their burden is very light.*

Like grain when it is threshed,
Like hay when it is mown,
Making, instead of more sense,
A music of its own:
> *Birdily, birdily bright*
> *Their burden is very light.*

A literary lyric poem is a song only metaphorically; it is designed to be spoken or read, and a formal refrain can often serve as a kind of reminder or substitute for an earlier relation to music. Some refrains are literal imitations of music—"fa la la la la," etc. Others may be a thematic phrase or sentence; the structural richness of refrains in modern verse depends upon one simple phenomenon: repeating something often may make it *more trivial*—because more expected and therefore carrying less information, as an engineer might put it—or, because of shifting or developing context in each stanza preceding, *more important.*

> What once was called a burden
> Was seldom heavy to bear.
> It was sung by the dancers, and heard in
> Between the stanzas, like air
> Rushing by between cars of a train,
> *Again and again and again.*

Like the point of a sharpened tool
Blunted by too much use,
Or a lesson learned in school
Drummed into the obtuse,
Here comes the old refrain
Again and again and again.

Like a sound from the distant past
Of remembered waves on a shore,
Each echo means more than the last,
Once more, once more and once more.
But *less* is more: too much is pain
Again and again and again.
(Like the pounding of hard rain
Again and again and again.)

(Bored with this dulling song,
Clever stanzas may set
Out on a walk less long,
Shift their burdens, and get
Each time, with the old refrain,
A gain and a gain and a gain.)

A BRIEF DIGRESSION: The three-beat accentual rhythm
of the last example reminds one of a problem men-
tioned at the beginning of this discussion, metrical
ambiguity. Keats's line ''How many bards gild the
lapses of time'' was given as an example; this latest
example of refrain suggests another, reminding us
how

Some lines like houses will—for ill or good—
Take on the look of a whole neighborhood,
Clearing muddles in which, alone, they stood.

As before, when we said a refrain
''Rushes by between cars of a train''—
All the anapests in it rang out
At the other ones gathered about.

But context governs, and will always reign:

"Rushing by between cars of a train"
Becomes a five-beat line without much pain.

But back to repetition. Two well-known forms, one from medieval Provence, one from France, delighted nineteenth-century makers of intricate verse and became important forms for meditative speculation in modern poetry. First, the *villanelle:*

This form with two refrains in parallel?
(Just watch the opening and the third line.)
The repetitions build the villanelle.

The subject thus established, it can swell
Across the poet-architect's design:
This form with two refrains in parallel

Must never make them jingle like a bell,
Tuneful but empty, boring and benign;
The repetitions build the villanelle

By moving out beyond the tercet's cell
(Though having two lone rhyme-sounds can confine
This form). With two refrains in parallel

A poem can find its way into a hell
Of ingenuity to redesign
The repetitions. Build the villanelle

Till it has told the tale it has to tell;
Then two refrains will finally intertwine.
This form with two refrains in parallel
The repetitions build: The Villanelle.

The other such form is the *sestina:* six stanzas, each of six lines, and a three-line *envoy* (or "send-off"), the repetition being not of lines, as in the villanelle, but of the terminal words of the lines of the first stanza:

Now we come to the complex *sestina:*
In the first stanza, each line's final word

Will show up subsequently at the ends
Of other lines, arranged in different ways;
The words move through the maze of a dark forest,
Then crash out, at the stanza's edge, to light.

The burden of repeating words is light
To carry through the course of a sestina;
And walking through the language of a forest
One comes on the clearing of an echoed word
Refreshingly employed in various ways,
Until one's amble through the stanza ends.

The next one starts out where the last one ends
As in the other cases, with the light
Sounds of two lines, like two roads or pathways
Meeting before they drift apart. Sestina
Patterns reveal the weaving ways a word
Can take through the thick clauses of a forest.

The poet dances slowly through a forest
Of permutations, a maze that never ends
(With seven hundred twenty ways those words
Can be disposed in six-line groups). But light
Falls through the leaves into the dark sestina
Picking out only six clear trails, six ways,

Like change-ringing in bells. The words find ways
And means for coping with an endless forest
By chopping out the course of a sestina.
Walking a known trail sometimes, one emends
The route a bit to skirt a green stone, light
With covering moss; or rings changes on words—

And so it is that the first stanza's word
Order—"Sestina," "Word," "End," and then "Ways"
(Three abstract, three concrete like "Forest," and "Light"
Which interweaves with leaves high in the forest)—
With the words' meanings serving different ends,
Repeats its pattern through the whole sestina.

Now the *envoy*'s last word: as the sestina's
End words make way for curtain calls, in the light
That floods the forest as the whole poem ends.

Some of the lyric forms from France remain a kind
of metric dance, without real poetry to say but good
for literary play (light verse, *vers de société*).

The *ballade* has only one refrain, but its three full
stanzas and short *envoy* are locked to the same
rhymes throughout.

> Where are the kinds of song that lay
> Along the medieval shore
> And then moved inland, light and gay,
> Still in the ancient garb they wore
> When speaking out of bed, and war,
> And François Villon's coughs and fleas?
> Where is their truth, their mighty roar?
> *Where are the old ballades like these?*
>
> Where are the eight-line stanzas' *a*
> *bab*, the beginning four
> Followed by quatrains which convey
> The *b*-rhyme that had sung before
> Its simple tune, in lines of yore?
> Where are the busy final *b*'s
> That make the old refrain implore
> *"Where are the old ballades like these?"*
>
> Where are the words that used to play,
> Wingèd, among the trees, and pour
> Old-fashioned rhyme, they hoped, for aye?
> Where's Rostand's rapier wit that tore
> Off bits of Cyrano's? Wherefore
> Did clever rhyming cease to please?
> Since jingle became a crashing bore
> *Where are the old ballades like these?*
>
> ENVOY
> Prince of Readers, I've ceased to soar:
> With rhymes used up, it's a tighter squeeze.
> The *envoy* ("send-off") asks, just once more,
> *Where are the old ballades like these?*

Another French lyric form, the *rondeau*, repeats only

part—the opening two iambic feet, usually—of its
first line:

> The rondeau's French in origin.
> For several centuries it's been
> Of use for light verse, in the main;
> Handling its lines can be the bane
> Of someone with an ear that's tin.
>
> The first words with which we begin
> Return, like a recurring sin—
> More Magdalen's than the crime of Cain.
> (The rondeau's French!)
>
> That's called the *rentrement*; and in
> The course of hearing these lines spin
> Themselves out, one may wait in vain
> For more rhymes, or a full refrain.
> With hardly any loss or gain
> English replaces, with a grin,
> The rondeau's French.

The *triolet* is the briefest of these, 5/8 of it being
composed of its two refrains:

> Triolets' second lines refrain
> From coming back until the end;
> Though the first one can cause some pain
> Triolets' second lines refrain
> From coming back yet once again.
> (The form's too fragile to offend.)
> Triolets' second lines refrain
> From coming back until the end.

The *pantoum* comes, through French again, from
Malay (*pantun*) and is rather like a combination of
villanelle with the unfolding motion of *terza rima* (p.
18). There may be any number of quatrains, but,
starting with the second one, they are generated by
repeating the even-numbered lines of each as the

odd-numbered ones of the next. The final line of the
poem repeats the opening one. In addition, a touch
of riddle is preserved in that the first half of each
quatrain is about something wholly different from
the second half. Thus:

> Ever so maddening in the *pantoum*,
> The repetitions frame a subtle doom.
> Evening has entered, her patches of gloom
> Now settled in the corners of the room.
>
> The repetitions frame a subtle doom:
> Each quatrain's first and third lines are refrains;
> Now settled-in, the corners of the room
> Attend the coming fever's chills and pains.
>
> Each quatrain's first and third lines are refrains,
> Returning from the previous second and fourth.
> Attend the coming fever's chills and pains!
> The wind is ominous, and from the north.
>
> Returning from the previous second and fourth,
> All these are complicated here by rhyme.
> The wind is ominous, and from the north—
> We talk about the weather half the time.
>
> All these are complicated here by rhyme
> Cleverly woven on the maker's loom.
> We talk about the weather half the time—
> Ever so maddening!—in the pantoum.

Another form based on refrain: that wonderful
modern mode of accentual oral poetry and song
called "The Blues." Musically, a 4/4 rhythm, usually
slow, moves through twelve measures in a fairly
fixed chordal sequence. [Musicians would identify
it as I (IV) I IV V I.] The repetition of the first line
is not merely decorative, nor expressive, as you will
see. Blues are improvised by the singer, like this:

Ballads from Scotland told stories and sang the news—
Ballads from Scotland told stories and sang the news,
  But black America felt and thought the blues.

Now a blues has stanzas, stanzas of a funny kind—
Yes a blues has stanzas of a very funny kind;
  (Do that line again, singer, while you make up your
    mind) . . .

Make up your mind, while the next line gives you time,
Make up your mind, yes, while this line's giving you time,
  Then your train of thought comes running after your
    rhyme.

You can quote a proverb; they say a new broom sweeps
    clean—
Yes, that's what they say: it's the new broom that sweeps
    clean,
  So sing a new line—make that proverb really *mean*.*

You sing the blues upside-down: you begin with the refrain—
O you sing upside-down, you start out with the refrain,
  And the end of a blues is like the falling rain.

—which leads one to remark that

In the words of "standards"—American popular song—
You'll find the germs
Of prosodical terms
Used in a way that sound a little wrong.

This whole introduction, for instance, is called the "verse";
The lines with the tune
That's familiar come soon
But who can remember *this* melody (that's its curse)

                              (or worse . . .)

* You see,
    Blues are like weddings, sad as a beat-up shoe
    Blues are like weddings, sad as a beat-up shoe
      With something borrowed, and something old or new.

  Blues are also witty, epigrammatic, and passionate at once.

But now for that A,A,B,A,
The pattern unrolling before us
In a very familiar way:
There are thirty-two bars to the chorus.

Whether crooned by some creature we love
Or by voices that threaten and bore us
Or by neither of the above,
There are thirty-two bars to the chorus.

There's new music for section B;
It's called the "release"—but from what?
—The burden of symmetry?
—The repeated eight bars that it's not?

This paradigm may have a ring
As passé as a big brontosaurus,
But we keep coming back to one thing:
There are thirty-two bars to the chorus.

Of brief, comical forms of verse which have become, in themselves, more like the formats for jokes,
the most celebrated is the *limerick*:

This most famous of forms is a fiddle
That we rub with a sexual riddle;
But the best of a *limerick*—
Though in Dutch or in Cymric—
Are the little short lines in the middle.

★

The mad limericks of one Edward Lear
Took a turn that was rather severe:
Their last rhymes—the same
As their first—were too tame.
That repetitive old Edward Lear!

The *clerihew*, invented by E(dmund) C(lerihew)
Bentley, is a skewed quatrain that frames a way of
turning rhyming jokes on names, and other jokes on
rhymes, and spoofing metrical neatness in the mode
of Ogden Nash (see page 30):

> A *clerihew*
> Will hardly transport you, or ferry you
> Over toward Parnassus
> (Better use some poetic Onassis).

Finally, a recent offshoot of the clerihew, invented by Anthony Hecht and first published by him in collaboration with this author: the *double-dactyl* is a pair of quatrains of two accentual dactyllic feet, with the following conditions placed on it:

> Starting with nonsense words
> ("Higgledy-piggledy"),
> Then comes a name
> (Making line number two);
>
> Somewhere along in the
> Terminal quatrain, a
> Didaktyliaios*
> Word, and we're through.

Or, in a perfect instance,

> Higgledy-piggledy
> Schoolteacher Hollanders
> Mutter and grumble and
> Cavil and curse,
>
> Hunting long words for the
> Antepenultimate
> Line of this light-weight but
> Intricate verse.

Before leaving scheme and figure of word and sound, we might remark that there are a number of rhetorical schemes associated with prose as well as with verse. We might consider a few of them that are commonly used in poetry. One of the most fa-

---

*Greek for "composed of two dactyls."

mous, and most important for early poetry, is the
so-called *epic simile*:

> Even as when some object familiar to us all—
> A street, a spoon, a river, a shoe, a star, a toothache—
> Is brought to our attention, called up from our memory
> To light up the darkened surface of something we've barely
>   known of
> —So did the epic simile sing of a silent past.

★

> *Zeugma*'s syntactic punning, sharp and terse,
> As on *in*'s senses, which we now rehearse:
> "Zeugma is used in earnest and this verse."

★

> *Anacoluthon* is a breaking-off
> Of what is being—a syntactic cough.

★

> *Apostrophe!* we thus address
> More things than I should care to guess.
> Apostrophe! I did invoke
> Your figure even as I spoke.

★

> *Anaphora* will repeat an opening phrase or word;
> Anaphora will pour it into a mould (absurd!);
> Anaphora will cast each subsequent opening;
> Anaphora will last until its tiring.
> Anaphora will seem to batter the hearer's mind,
> Anaphora will make mere likeness seem unkind;
> Anaphora will sound like some rhetorical fault,
> Anaphora will be reformed by Whitman, Walt.
> Or else it can caress you with a gentle hand
> Or else it can be text for hope to understand,
> Or else it can become a kind of incantation,
> Or else it can shape up into a proclamation.

★

> *Homoeoteleuton* is the opposite: like ending,
> Where the same word will make a similar ending

Or, perhaps, as in Latin, a chunk of case-ending,
Or, as in English, a participial —ing,
Or even, if you wish, and perhaps bending
The usual sense of it, a rhyming sort of ending.

Chiasmus is a general scheme of patterning two pairs of elements; its name is derived from the Greek letter χ (*chi*); in English, we might call it X-ing. Its elements can be merely those of paired vowel-sounds, as in

Resounding syllables

In simple nouns.

Or the crossing can be one of syntactical elements,

Echoing adjectives,

And nouns resounding.

Or, muting the funny sound of inversion for modern ears with its archaic and heroic cast, we can do as Milton did, and enjamb the adjectival participle to modify the grammar:

Echoing adjectives and nouns resounding
Deep in the draughty vastness of a scheme.

Or the crossing can arrange particular words, as in

Imagined mirrors mirror imagining

or this:

Speech which in part reflects on parts of speech

—or even a metaphoric pattern, although here we touch on realms of trope, not scheme; an example which interlaces syntax and image leaves the penultimate word cast as noun and adjective:

The burning darkness and the *light* freezing.

Other schemes of placement were never classified
by rhetoricians, perhaps because they only came up
in English verse and in the context of English word
order. The way in which a pair of adjectives modi-
fying the same noun can be arranged, for example,
has consequence for our verse. For

> Polysyllabic long words, preceding short ones,
>   deliver
> Adjectival, sharp blows
>   to the
>   modified next noun.

On the other hand, for example, we learn by scan-
ning a pattern of

> Coupled adjectives dynamic,

of their

> Slower disclosure and instructive.

> ★

> Thus, at the end of an iambic line,
> This scheme could find a lasting place, and fine.

We conclude with a general afterthought,

> Let us talk of variation:
> In a very boring meter
> Like this blank (unrhymed) trochaic
> —Four beats, so *tetrameter*—the
> Chance for any subtle rhythm
> To develop, making any
> Line sound much more like itself than
> Like the others all around it
> Isn't very high at all (a
> Cycle written in this verse form
> By the poet Henry Wadsworth
> Longfellow—it's most well known—is
> Called *The Song of Hiawatha*,

Imitated from the Finnish
Meter of an epic cycle
Called—in Finnish—*Kalevala*.

But let us move into a form—
Iambic, with four beats the norm—
And listen to the way that lines
Tap out their rhythms, while designs
Of rhyme and reason, overlaid
On the straight tune that's being played
Can make these lines (although they rhyme)
Less like a clock that ticks the time
Or wakes us up with an alarming chime.
Lines may be varied with a rare
Misplaced syllable here and there,
Even two beats together, strong
Enough to shove their words along
The line a bit, until they drop
Into the next, and finally stop.
Rhythms can shimmer, just like this;
Two lines can delicately kiss;
Some words' slow burdens make them bleed
And, fudged, bunched, clustered, hurt to read;
Each line can echo what it says;
Yet family resemblances
Still hold between the various faces
Of lines in their respective places.

The effects of sound observed in the preceding lines represent a more general matter, that of so-called "imitative sound" or, more technically, "verbal mimesis." In its own way, this is a kind of myth-making at the smallest level, and can be considered not so much a scheme or pattern, but a mode of trope itself: the myth is one of semantic presence in a place of nonreferential sound (or, as some might want to put it, a natural relation occurring in a conventional one that has, indeed, just been established in the verse). Thus,

Technical mastery should not astound—
The sense must seem an echo to the sound,
And verse can be a charm to conjure up
A ghost of meaning in an empty cup,
That nymph the linguists call "Morpheme"—a naiad
Of sense—from out a cell of sound. This triad:
"The fires of autumn dwindle to December,
A spark of meaning hides in its grey ember
And kindles in its name what we remember"
—Illustrates well the point: nothing in *e*'s
M's and *b*'s means "residual." But these
Are tropes, like rhyme, purporting to have found
In a mere accident of common sound
A hidden jewel of meaning, hard and bright,
Bred by the pressure of the ear's delight.
Thus: *m*-sounds can feel flabbier or firmer
When heard in "mime," or overheard in "murmur";
There's nothing in that general object, *it*,
That suits it for its role in "spit" or "shit"
(Low comedy), or, properly, in "fit."
H's are only breathless when in "hoarse"
("Horses" run smoothly from the start, of course).
Sl as in "slip" and "slap" and "sleet" and "slide"
Etcetera, perhaps connotes a glide
Of unimpeded motion; I suppose
That stuffed, initial *sn* suggests the nose.
But mostly, all these morphophonemes that
Poetry seems to pull out of its hat
Are verse's metaphors of having found
Buried significance in natural ground.

SUGGESTIONS FOR
FURTHER READING

Readers who are not already familiar with my great original should acquaint themselves with Pope's heuristic, self-descriptive verses in *An Essay on Criticism*, lines 337–83. Spenser, Coleridge, Tennyson, and Robert Bridges all wrote metrical experiments and examples, which can be found in their collected works. Wordsworth, Keats, and Dante Gabriel Rossetti have sonnets on the subject of the sonnet. Karl Shapiro's *An Essay on Rime* is in verse, with some self-descriptive bits. In French, Vincent Voiture (1598–1648) wrote a famous rondeau on how to write a rondeau.

Paul Fussell's *Poetic Meter and Poetic Form* (rev. ed., New York, 1979) is an excellent discursive introduction to some of the problems of prosodic analysis. The essays in Harvey Gross, ed., *The Structure of Verse: Modern Essays on Prosody* (rev. ed., New York, 1979) cover an array of problems and views. My own *Vision and Resonance* (New York, 1975) includes discussions of formal problems of a more specialized nature. Two brilliant essays of the late W. K. Wimsatt underlie most contemporary discussions: "One Relation of Rhyme to Reason," in *The Verbal Icon* (Lexington, Ky., 1954) and "In Search of Verbal Mimesis," in *The Day of the Leopards* (New Haven, 1976). Wimsatt also edited a most valuable handbook of comparative metrics called *Versification: Major Language Types* (New York, 1972); pp. 191–252 are devoted to English prosody and its problems. Individual entries in the *Princeton Encyclopedia of Poetry and Poetics* (enlarged ed., Princeton, 1974) of metrical interest include larger discussions such as "Meter," "Prosody," "Verse and Prose," "Music and Poetry," "Song," "Concrete Poetry," etc., as well as essays on many national literatures, East and West. In addition there is a multitude of smaller notes on particular forms, prosodic terms, etc. George Saintsbury's *A History of English Prosody from the Twelfth Century to the Present Day* is exhaustive and slow-paced; the portion of it reprinted as *Historical Manual of English Prosody* will probably be more useful to all but a handful of specialists.

More limited in scope and subject are such studies as those of Derek Attridge on quantitative verse in English—*Well-Weigh'd Syllables* (Cambridge, 1976)—or Helen Louise Cohen, *Lyric Forms from France* (New York, 1922). Harvey Gross, *Sound and Form in Modern Poetry* (Ann Arbor, 1964), and John Thompson, *The Founding of English Metre* (New York, 1961), shed reasonable light on obscure questions. Robert Bridges, *Milton's Prosody* (Oxford, 1921), and Edward M. Weismiller, "Studies of Verse Form in the Minor English Poems," in *A Variorum Commentary on the Poems of John Milton* II, pt. 3 (New York, 1972), both raise important general questions. Donald Wesling, *The Chances of Rhyme: Device and Modernity* (Berkeley and Los Angeles, 1980), is brief and provocative; T. S. Omond, *English Metrists*, is an ultimately amusing account of the contentions and pedantries of prosodic theorists in English. Catherine Ing, in *Elizabethan Lyrics* (London, 1951), pays some illuminating attention to the relations between verse and musical structures, and Elise B. Jorgens, *Let Well-Tun'd Words Amaze* (Minneapolis, 1981), examines in detail the transformation of verse into song in the seventeenth century. George Puttenham's *The Arte of English Poesie* (1589) is still of great interest for both prosody and rhetoric, the latter of which is cleverly and usefully served by Richard A. Lanham, *A Handbook of Rhetorical Terms* (Berkeley and Los Angeles, 1969). For transcendent afterthoughts on many of these matters, Justus George Lawler's *Celestial Pantomime* (New Haven, 1979) is remarkable, but cannot be recommended to beginners.